DIGITAL AND INFORMATION LITERACY™

NET NEUTRALITY AND WHAT IT MEANS TO YOU

JEFF MAPUA

rosen publishing's
rosen central®

New York

Published in 2017 by The Rosen Publishing Group, Inc.
29 East 21st Street, New York, NY 10010

Library of Congress Cataloging-in-Publication Data

Names: Mapua, Jeff, author.
Title: Net neutrality and what it means to you / Jeff Mapua.
Description: First Edition. New York : Rosen Central, 2017. | Series: Digital and information literacy | Includes bibliographical references and index. |
Identifiers: LCCN 2016017421| ISBN 9781499465136 (library bound) | ISBN 9781499465112 (pbk.) | ISBN 9781499465129 (6-pack)
Subjects: LCSH: Internet governance—Juvenile literature. | Telecommunication policy—Juvenile literature.
Classification: LCC TK5105.8854 .M37 2017 | DDC 384.3—dc23
LC record available at https://lccn.loc.gov/2016017421

Manufactured in China

CONTENTS

INTRODUCTION

On February 13, 2016, Justice of the Supreme Court Antonin Scalia passed away. His death left an open seat on the Supreme Court. A new judge will take Scalia's place. The Supreme Court is the highest court in the judicial branch of government and its rulings affect laws across the United States. The Democrats want a Democratic judge to fill the empty spot. Likewise, Republicans prefer a Republican. They care so much because judges' political beliefs greatly influence their decisions. Each political party hopes that the new nominee will echo their own beliefs.

The open Supreme Court seat comes at a time when companies often fight government decisions. One such agency is the Federal Communications Commission. Also called the FCC, it regulates US media communications. This includes the internet, TV, and radio. It also oversees cell phone traffic. The case *Arlington v. FCC* made it to the Supreme Court. It involved the building of wireless phone towers. Justice Scalia and Chief Justice John Roberts, another Republican, disagreed on their rulings. Roberts said that Scalia's choice to side with the FCC created a dangerous precedent. The FCC might impose other rules at any time, he argued. Scalia believed that the FCC did nothing wrong. He said they were using the power they already had.

Laws about what businesses and everyday people can and cannot do with media are changing all the time. The debate over net neutrality is a

Associate Justice of the Supreme Court Antonin Scalia, a long-time conservative, was appointed to the bench in 1986 and served until his death in 2016.

debate over how the internet is run at its most basic level. The internet must be accessed through a connection controlled by service providers. This gives service providers a lot of power since they decide what an internet user can see.

Justice Scalia's replacement will rule on net neutrality cases. Activists will continue to fight to keep the internet as it is today. Other groups will try to adapt the online world for their benefit. How this struggle plays out has the power to affect every internet user in the United States.

Chapter 1

Battle for the Internet

The internet is everywhere. It used to be confined to computers on a desk. Now people can access it through smartphones, smart cars, smart televisions, and more. The internet has changed the way people work, talk, and consume media and entertainment. People from around the world are instantly connected like never before.

Because the internet is so ever present, a lot of people care about how it is run. This often brings companies, activist groups, and the government in conflict.

What Is Net Neutrality?

When the internet was introduced, users could log on and visit any site they wanted. Each site and service worked exactly the same. If a student was doing research on an online encyclopedia and then visited a shopping site, both sites were treated the same on the network.

Unlike the early days of computers, today the internet is accessible by many different devices such as smartphones and tablets.

How the Internet Works

A network is a number of interconnected things. They can be computers, machines, or operations. Many offices, homes, and schools have computer networks inside a single building. The Internet is a worldwide network of computers.

Every house has its own address. So does each computer on the internet. This is called an IP address. "IP" stands for "Internet Protocol." Each computer's IP address is unique. Computers can communicate with each another by knowing their IP addresses.

Computers access the internet through an internet service provider, or ISP. It usually charges customers a monthly fee. In the United States, there are many ISPs. They include AT&T, Comcast, Time Warner, Verizon, and more. Each computer on the internet is assigned an IP address.

Who Controls the Internet?

At the beginning, the internet was an open network. All sites were seen as the same. But as technology has advanced, companies have changed how the internet is accessed. These changes can help raise a company's profits. They can also improve their customers' experience. Some security measures protect users from computer viruses.

IP Blocking

One method for limiting internet access is called IP blocking. It involves blocking connections from a specific IP address or range of addresses. Usually this is done because these addresses may be harmful to users. If a network administrator believes that a computer with a certain IP address is hostile, that IP address is kept from connecting to that network's machines.

Entire countries can practice IP blocking, too. This is a cheap, quick solution that is generally the first step in internet filtering. But this can lead to overblocking. Safe sites could also be blocked.

Many countries practice IP blocking. China obstructs access to at least three hundred IP addresses. These addresses are blocked across all ISPs. Azerbaijan, Ethiopia, India, Jordan, Libya, Pakistan, and South Korea block IP addresses, too.

Bandwidth Throttling

ISPs can also use bandwidth throttling to control a user's access to sites. The company Comcast often uses this practice. It slows down the connection speed of specific users. Connection speed is how fast information travels to

The internet can be monitored by a country's government and controlled. Different governments have different ideas about what information should be free and what should be restricted.

and from a user. This is done because these users slow the network. Some people think throttling is a bad solution to busy networks. Instead, they think that the networks should be designed better to begin with.

In 2008, a complaint was filed against Comcast. It stated that the company violated users' rights to an open internet by using this tactic. Comcast argued that some users overloaded the network's capacity. They believed that bandwidth throttling was necessary. If they did not do it, then other users' connection speeds would be slowed down. The FCC ordered Comcast to stop this practice.

Content Selection

ISPs can also limit access to sites based on content. This could be done to shield users from illegal or unlawful material found online. This kind of filtering

Comcast vans like these are frequent sights in many neighborhoods since the company is a popular provider of media and internet service. In 2008, Comcast tested the US government's commitment to upholding network neutrality.

can be done on a small scale. Examples of this are blocking software installed on home or office computers. It can also be done on a wider scale by ISPs.

One example of this occurred in the early 2000s. An ISP called Madison River Communications limited site access. It kept customers from visiting

---

File   Edit   View   Favorites   Tools   Help

ZERO-RATING

Zero-Rating

Zero-rating involves ISPs charging customers for certain kinds of data. One example of this can be specific applications. Another can be online services on an ISP's network. ISPs and wireless service providers limit customer data. That is, they offer product plans that restrict how much data a customer can use in a certain time period. For example, a company can let a customer download a set amount of data from the internet each month. One song can be around 5 megabytes, while one movie can be over 1,000 mega-bytes, or one gigabyte. Once the customer reaches that limit, the company may stop service or charge more until the next month begins.

Zero-rating is a way for ISPs to mark certain applications or websites as "free" or exempt from a customer's data usage. One service that uses a lot of data is streaming videos. A customer's data use is often affected by fre-quent video streaming. If an ISP has its own streaming service, it can choose to let customers use that service for free. It could also decide that access to other streaming services should "cost" more. That means that it could use up customers' data plans quicker.

Zero-rating is legal in the United States. However, the government has warned that these services will be closely watched. In Canada, mobile carri-ers cannot zero-rate their own services. Other countries such as the Netherlands, Slovenia, and Chile have also banned it.

competing services. One such competitor offered phone services competing with their own services. In 2005, the FCC stepped in to halt this practice.

How Will It Affect Internet Users?

Since the beginning of the internet, controls over what a user can see and do have evolved. These controls were loose at first but are now tightening up. Such changes can be seen as threats to net neutrality. In general, net neutrality describes a network with absolute equality. This means the quality of service users pay for should be the same. Supporters of net neutrality accept that ISPs can vary the quality of service based on consumer trends. They object to charging fees to do so, though.

FCC Chairman Tom Wheeler provided testimony to the US Senate to defend net neutrality. The FCC has been a major player in the use and regulation of internet service in the United States.

When ISPs ignore net neutrality, users may have lower internet connection speeds. For example, videos online can become harder to access. The connection speed can cause a poor viewing experience. Or the videos can be interrupted entirely. The ISP often claims that a third party is causing problems in network traffic, and the end users suffer for it. In other words, the ISP is not responsible for the network quality. But access to certain sites can be perfectly fine. While not technically blocked from all sites on the internet, the user has an economic boundary. An economic boundary is a barrier based on money instead of a physical thing like a wall or fence. If users only access their preferred sites, they will use up more data than those who access zero-rated websites or services. They then will have to pay extra once they exceed their data.

In other cases, those users who pay higher fees can have faster, more reliable service than those who pay less. The higher fees provide a sort of internet "fast lane," where they are allowed to access faster service than other users. For those who can afford it, the internet remains easy to access and frustration free.

The Story Until Now

In the United States, the debate over net neutrality was addressed by the FCC in February 2015. A document called the Open Internet Order outlined three "bright-line" rules. ISPs and mobile broadband providers must follow these rules. It states that there is to be no blocking, no throttling, and no paid prioritization.

No blocking means that ISPs cannot block access to lawful content, applications, and services. Devices that are "nonharmful" must be given access to the ISP network. The no-throttling rule means that service cannot be slowed down by the ISP. Finally, no paid prioritization means that ISPs cannot create "internet fast lanes" or toll lanes. This means a company cannot pay an ISP to provide faster services to their particular site or application.

While the FCC has made their stance on net neutrality clear, the battle for the internet is far from over. There have been many challenges since February 2015. They are sure to continue happening in the future as well. Consumers may prefer to pay for special services, too. Online privacy and data collection are also new twists in the net neutrality debate.

MYTHS & FACTS

MYTH The internet was always neutral.

FACT Spam and other potential threats have existed since the early years of the Internet.

MYTH Net neutrality means all connection speeds are the same.

FACT ISPs offer different connection speeds for business service versus residential service.

MYTH The internet and the World Wide Web are the same.

FACT The internet is a large series of networks, and the World Wide Web is just one of many systems used to connect to this network.

14

Chapter 2

The Two Sides

Many people are for neutrality and many are against it. The US government has chosen to support it. But there are still many questions facing the FCC. Supporters say that the FCC is not following its own rules. Opponents say that the government has tried to do too much.

Many groups are interested in how the internet will be controlled. These include ISPs, government officials, content providers, and general users.

Yes to Neutrality

Those who support net neutrality want an internet where all websites, applications, and programs have the same priority. Net neutrality tries to maintain how the internet has worked from the start. It also supports small companies. How does it do this? By giving them an equal chance to find success. Bigger companies do not always have an advantage. Supporters want the FCC to watch over ISPs to make sure they follow the rules.

Preserving the Internet

Supporters believe that the internet should treat all data equally. ISPs build the network with their businesses. They lack control over what passes through it. Those same providers were not allowed to charge companies more money to send their data faster than other companies. To supporters, the internet works like a democracy. They want it to be equal for everyone.

Those for neutrality compare the internet to a landline phone system. The phone company builds the lines and cables that connect phones to one another. They cannot lower the quality of certain phone calls. They also cannot end a call if they don't like whom a person is speaking to.

Without net neutrality, internet users may have to pay extra to access websites such as popular video provider YouTube.

Most agree that the internet was neutral in its early days. But those who fight neutrality say it has changed over time. They say that some websites have become too popular. They use an unfair amount of the network.

File   Edit   View   Favorites   Tools   Help

NETFLIX AND STREAMING MEDIA

Netflix and Streaming Media

Netflix began as a company that rented out DVDs to customers. They were sent through the mail. At the time this was unusual. Rental stores like Blockbuster and Hollywood Video had physical addresses. Netflix then introduced video streaming in addition. Customers could now rent movies without heading out to the store. They did not need to wait for DVDs in the mail either.

The move to streaming services was a huge success. By 2013, 30 percent of all traffic on the Internet was on Netflix. Netflix came out in support of net neutrality. The company argued before the FCC for months. They said that ISPs needed to be watched closely. Otherwise, net neutrality could be compromised. Over time, this stance won out.

Later, though, Netflix changed their practices. The company's chief financial officer, David Wells, made an interesting statement. He said they disagreed with the government's net neutrality ruling. Netflix seemed to have switched sides. Then in early 2015, they made a deal in Australia. Netflix would now be zero-rated. Users there would no longer see their data quickly used up if they visited Netflix. This violated net neutrality rules.

Netflix argues that they are playing by the laws of Australia. Where does the company stand on neutrality then? Many fear that the net neutrality ally is now an opponent.

Even Playing Field

Those supporting net neutrality say that smaller companies need it. It will allow them to compete against bigger companies. They could suffer if ISPs can charge companies like Netflix or Hulu a fee to ensure better service for users. Without protection, ISPs can charge companies that stream content, such as YouTube, an extra fee. This fee would buy better service for customers. People could watch their videos without them stopping or skipping. But not all companies might be able to afford that fee. People would choose the better service. It would come from the company with more money. Smaller companies would lose out in the end.

Notable Supporters

In May 2014, over one hundred companies wrote a letter to the FCC and its chairman, Tom Wheeler. They wrote to support net neutrality. The letter said that the internet was always neutral. Many large companies signed it. Those companies included Amazon, Dropbox, eBay, Etsy, Facebook, Google, Kickstarter, LinkedIn, Microsoft, Netflix, Reddit, Tumblr, Twitter, and Yahoo!.
     The letter talked about net neutrality and internet control issues. The companies were against ISPs breaking neutrality. They say it is vital. It will keep the internet a place "for free speech and opportunity for billions of users." President Barack Obama and US senators Bernie Sanders and Elizabeth Warren have been big supporters.

No to Neutrality

Those against net neutrality have their own reasons. They say that they want low costs for users. They also want innovation. Finally, they want fast connection speeds. But at what cost?

The price for using the internet could go up due to net neutrality, leaving many consumers with less in their wallets.

Rising Costs

Opponents argue that net neutrality raises prices. They want lower prices to get onto the internet. They say ISPs could get more money by charging content providers extra fees. These fees pay for faster connections. For example, ISPs expect to earn money each month. Music or video sites might use these ISPs. They want to provide good services to their customers. Part of this includes fast internet speeds. ISPs can charge these content providers a fee each month. This fee would give customers the fastest possible speeds.

Like traffic jams, internet service can slow down from too many users online at the same time. Slow internet connections can be a source of major frustration.

ISPs now have extra money. They can then lower the prices they charge internet users. Now they get their income from content providers.

Experts think this is a good option. They say charging content providers gives people lower bills. But there's a problem with this model. It depends on the ISPs reducing users' bills. What if they continue to charge customers the same amount? They could decide to keep this extra money. Nothing would prevent them from doing that.

Content providers may also raise the cost of their services. They could say they need extra money to pay the ISPs. Streaming websites may decide to charge their customers a monthly fee. Customers could see higher bills.

Anti-Innovation

ISPs can keep the money from charging content providers. They do not have to lower prices for their customers. ISPs can also use the extra money in another way. They could make their services even better.

For example, an ISP could use the money to update their network. They could then serve more people at the same time. ISPs could also help their workers create new designs, or innovate. Many people believe that companies should be able to make as much money as possible. Losing money because of net neutrality hurts innovation.

Service providers also see competition between each other as a good thing. It encourages people to invent new ways to give better services. Letting companies charge more will force them to create new ideas to beat their competitors.

Less Traffic and Faster Speeds

ISPs serve a greater number of people than ever before. But the networks that connect to the internet are suffering. Too many people get online at the same time. Just as when there are too many cars on a highway, this causes heavy traffic on the network. The ISP's customers connect to what is called a local access network. This is where traffic or congestion occurs. Those against net neutrality say that giving all users the same access is not the best way to use a network.

Most ISPs want to charge customers for better internet access. They have outlined plans for this. They show that some websites will work better than others. This means that if an online retailer or content provider pays a fee, their site will have better connection speeds at all times. Critics say that ISPs have not proven their case to the FCC. They doubt that traffic actually occurs on local access networks.

Notable Opponents

On December 10, 2014, a letter went out to the FCC, Chairman Tom Wheeler, and the US Congress. More than sixty technology companies signed it. They opposed net neutrality. They fought the proposal to classify the internet as a utility, like water or electricity. Costs of such a proposal would damage them and their employees, they said.

Some companies that signed the letter are Cisco, dLink, Ericsson, IBM, Intel, MetroTel, Nokia, Panasonic, and Qualcomm. They said that net neutrality would keep them from improving their networks. Financial struggles would prevent them from investing in ways to provide better services. Other opponents include AT&T, Comcast, and Verizon. Kentucky senator Rand Paul and former Florida governor Jeb Bush also opposed it.

TEN GREAT QUESTIONS
TO ASK AN INTERNET POLICY EXPERT

1 How will network neutrality affect my everyday web surfing?

2 Will net neutrality change the cost of using the internet?

3 How will the internet change with net neutrality rules in place?

4 Why should I care if there is net neutrality or not?

5 What does it mean to regulate the internet?

6 Will the economy be affected by net neutrality?

7 Is net neutrality a right or a privilege?

8 What do different political parties think of net neutrality?

9 How can the FCC control my access to the internet?

10 Is it currently legal for ISPs to charge companies for better connection speeds?

Chapter 3

Net Neutrality Around the World

Net neutrality affects people all over the world, not just in the United States. The internet is a global tool. Every country must address net neutrality. Some countries have taken strong steps to protect it. Other countries have taken steps to break it. Many countries have not yet made a decision one way or the other. The result is a world with different levels of it in place. This leaves the question of global net neutrality unanswered today and maybe for years to come.

World's First Neutrality in Chile

In 2010, Chile became the first country in the world to pass a law to protect net neutrality. It is called the Net Neutrality Law. The law said ISPs could not control their network. This means they cannot block or choose which sites get fast connection speeds. ISPs cannot stop users from seeing content, applications, or legal services on their network. The law said that ISPs' connection plans had to be open for everyone to see. The law also let customers request parental controls.

After three years of discussions, the law was finally passed. It received positive responses from the general public. The law was promoted by a group of citizens. The group was known as Neutralidad Sí. They urged their representatives to pass the neutrality law. They wanted to guarantee internet users' rights. They also showed that ISPs were already practicing blocking.

But the law did not make all groups happy. The exact wording of the law was not strong enough for everyone. The law said ISPs cannot "arbitrarily" block legal content. But if an ISP does not block content arbitrarily, they could then discriminate against certain websites without getting into trouble.

Neutrality in Europe

In October 2015, the European Union, or EU, held a vote on a set of rules. The rules were written to protect net neutrality for countries in the EU. There were already rules on how internet traffic was managed in Europe. The new rules were meant to make net neutrality stronger. They include placing rules on zero-rating agreements. There are also rules for fast and slow lanes for users.

The World Wide Web was invented by Sir Tim Berners-Lee. He did this in 1989 while employed at CERN, the European Organization for Nuclear Research.

Several companies, including Netflix, Reddit, and Vimeo, fought for the new rules. The inventor of the

World Wide Web is a man named Sir Tim Berners-Lee. He also came out in favor of the neutrality rules. But the EU voted to reject all the new rules. The vote was a big victory for opponents of net neutrality.

Sir Tim Berners-Lee

The man credited with inventing the World Wide Web is Sir Tim-Berners Lee. He was born in London, England, on June 8, 1955. Tim was the oldest of four children. He was the first son born to mathematicians and computer pioneers Conway Berners-Lee and Mary Lee Woods. Tim inherited his parents' interest in computers.

Tim continued to follow his interest in computers through school. He did well in math and science subjects. But not many schools offered computer science classes. While in college at Oxford, Berners-Lee used one of the few computers available for a prank. He was then banned from using it. That did not stop Berners-Lee from learning about computers. He built his own computer using whatever spare parts he could find. This included an old adding machine he found in the dumpster at the sawmill where he worked.

Berners-Lee earned a degree in physics from Oxford. Afterward he found work as a software engineer. He eventually landed a job working with computers at CERN. CERN was the world's largest particle physics laboratory. He began work on a new system called Enquire. The system would track everything happening at CERN. This project led him to creating what is now known as the World Wide Web. It was based on a concept called hypertext (the "ht" in "http"). The World Wide Web became available Christmas Day 1990. Tim has been a protector of the internet ever since.

Other countries in the EU already have net neutrality laws in place. These countries are the Netherlands, Slovenia, and Finland. Their laws would have to be changed to agree with the current neutrality laws.

Neutrality in India

Facebook introduced a program in India called Free Basics in 2016. Indian mobile provider Reliance would provide the program. Free Basics was soon banned by the Indian government. The program was advertised by Facebook as a way to provide free mobile service to hundreds of millions of people in three dozen countries. It would also bring cheap Wi-Fi to rural Indian villages. Facebook founder Mark Zuckerberg wrote an article for the

Facebook founder Mark Zuckerberg's attempt to give internet access to millions of Indians was thwarted by network neutrality activists.

Times of India. He said that free Internet is a basic service for society, like education.

Net neutrality activists rallied against the program. They pointed out that Free Basics would have given free access to only a select part of the internet. This included Facebook. Neutrality supporters said that Free Basics operated on a zero-rating model. It gave Facebook the power to shape the information available to everyone on the program. More than eight hundred thousand Indians sent emails to the Telecom Regulatory Authority of India (TRAI) to complain about Free Basics. Many Indian companies and businesses backed out of the program because of the public pressure.

The TRAI's decision was officially a part of regulations called the Prohibition of Discriminatory Tariffs for Data Services Regulations 2016. The

In 2016, net neutrality activists in India protested Facebook's Free Basics program. Their outspoken criticism was taken seriously.

regulations say that service providers cannot charge extra for data services based on content. They also made any special arrangements to do so illegal. Another mobile provider called Airtel had a similar program to Free Basics called Airtel Zero. Airtel was also banned from releasing it. Neutrality supporters are now fighting to ban ISPs from controlling connection speeds to websites based on content.

Brazil

Brazil is the largest economy in South America. The country passed a law in 2014 that guarantees net neutrality. The law is known as Marco Civil or "Internet Bill of Rights." Telecommunications companies are not allowed to

In 2014 there were over 600 million Chinese internet users, making them the largest online population in the world. The number of users is likely to increase in the coming years.

change prices based on how much content users access. The law limits how much the government or ISPs can interfere with internet usage. Marco Civil protects consumer privacy by limiting how much information the government can collect.

Privacy concerns were the driving force behind net neutrality. In 2013, a scandal revealed to the world that the US government was spying on US citizens. Brazil responded by making Marco Civil a top priority. A petition of 344,000 signatures showed how important the issue was to Brazilians. People there spend more time online than watching television.

However, the progress made toward net neutrality was not enough for everyone. Supporters say that Marco Civil still falls short of protecting the internet. The law allows websites to keep data about consumers for six months. This raises concerns about privacy. Also ISPs could be slowing down service. This is against neutrality rules.

China

China is one of the world's biggest economies. They have a large amount of wealth and resources. The Chinese people make up the world's largest internet population. There were more than 648 million internet users in China at the end of 2014. Reporters Without Borders is a nonprofit organization. It classified China as an "Enemy of the Internet" for its vast censoring and blocking. Many countries control the internet for economic reasons. China controls the internet for political reasons. They target many kinds of websites. Common targets are anything that can be seen as politically or socially sensitive.

The Communist government in China wields an extreme level of power. This includes power over the internet and communications. The service providers are all owned and run by the government. The government can control what content the Chinese people can and cannot access. Weibo is a popular microblogging platform in China. Weibo provided relatively uncensored news and information. The government placed rules that hurt the site by blocking its content. Weibo saw fewer people use the site after the rules were introduced.

China uses a powerful filtering system. It can block tens of thousands of websites. It blocks websites based on web address and keyword censoring. This system has come to be known as the Great Firewall of China. It filters both Chinese and foreign content. Popular websites such as Facebook, Twitter, and YouTube are blocked. Human rights websites are also blocked. There are thousands of cyberpolice in China who watch the Internet and monitor internet cafes.

Chapter 4

Keeping the Net Free for All

How is neutrality handled in the United States? Other countries have already endured neutrality challenges by global sites such as Facebook. There is a wide range of internet control in the world. The direction in which the United States chooses to proceed will be a hotly debated decision.

Neutrality in the United States

Democrats are generally in favor of neutrality. Republicans are generally against it. There are exceptions either way. Just how the internet can or cannot be regulated has been an ongoing legal battle that began in the early 2000s. ISPs, who built their networks, wanted websites like Google to pay for using them. Starting in 2007, Comcast and the FCC battled back and forth. The issue they fought over was throttling connection speeds for users of an application called BitTorrent. BitTorrent is a popular file-sharing program. Eventually the president had to weigh in on the issue.

The White House has publicly supported net neutrality, but since different parties have different positions, that could change under a new president.

The White House's Stance

In 2014, the net neutrality debate began to attract more attention than ever before. President Barack Obama made it clear that he supported an open internet. He stated that the internet was created neutral. He said it is an essential part of the American economy. His support, though, did not finish the debate. In 2010, the FCC passed rules called the Open Internet Order that were designed to protect net neutrality. Obama said that the rules had as little impact on ISPs and telecommunications companies as possible. One such company is Verizon. It sells cell phones and service plans for them and an array of internet services. Verizon sued the FCC, stating that it did not have the authority to enforce these rules. They appealed to the US Court of Appeals for the D.C. Circuit. Verizon won. It was ruled that the FCC did not have the power to set those rules. During his time in office, Obama continued to push for net neutrality. He outlined "bright-line" rules for ISPs.

The first of these rules banned blocking by ISPs. Obama thought that all legal content should have equal access regardless of company affiliation. The second rule declared that ISPs could not throttle some content and speed up others. Third, Obama called for increased openness between ISPs and the rest of the open network. This was designed to stop special treatment between service providers and content providers. Lastly, there would be no paid prioritization and similar restrictions. Obama's goal was to keep an even playing field for all companies. Soon, a new version of the Open Internet Order would be introduced.

The Open Internet Order

In February 2015, the FCC approved a net neutrality policy by a close 3-2 vote. The policy is called the Open Internet Order, and it replaced the 2010 version. It addresses what ISPs are allowed to do with their networks. The Open Internet Order replaced a 2010 version. These rules had been greatly challenged. The FCC tried to reclassify broadband as a public utility. This would enable them to regulate ISPs. They were able to do just that with some ISPs. These are classified as carriers under Title II of the Telecommunications Act. The new policy bans blocking, throttling, and paid-prioritization fast lanes. These rules also extend to mobile devices and companies that provide mobile services.

The order was reached only after a hostile battle. Many activists and companies on both sides pled their cases. Julie Veach is chief of the FCC's Wireline Competition Bureau. She reported that four million Americans commented on the neutrality vote. Several people who work in the

Cell phone towers help people communicate around the world. When you turn on your phone it sends a message that is picked up by the tower's antennae.

File   Edit   View   Favorites   Tools   Help

TITLE II

Title II

Title II refers to the Communications Act of 1934. The 1934 Act created the FCC. It outlined the FCC's power to regulate communications and broadcasting. The FCC can regulate ISPs only if the internet is classified as a "common carrier." Reclassifying it would give the FCC power over it. It would be like the power it has over television and radio. The FCC would then force ISPs to act "in the public interest."

Title II states that common carriers cannot "make any unjust or unreasonable discrimination in charges, practices, classifications, regulations, facilities, or services." This would then apply to ISPs. The Communications Act of 1934 is over eighty years old. Many fear it is outdated. Technology has changed greatly since 1934. The laws were updated in 1996. But even neutrality advocates admit that such an update is not ideal.

telecommunications industry spoke in support of the order. Chad Dickerson, CEO of commerce website Etsy, defended neutrality. Veena Sud, writer and producer of the Netflix show *The Killing*, also spoke. She described how her show survived with the help of online video streaming. Sir Tim Berners-Lee, creator of the World Wide Web, created a short video that was also shown in support.

The two Republicans who voted were against the order. Michael O'Rielly and Ajit Pai warned that the FCC was going beyond its authority. Pai worried that the FCC was disturbing commerce and restricting internet freedom. Passing the order was a "radical departure" from past actions, he said. He believed they were passing it only because the president pushed for it. Higher costs for internet use might result. Less innovation by business could also occur.

The group Broadband for America, with members from major ISPs, asked Congress to intervene. The cochairs of the group were John Sununu and Harold Ford Jr. They claimed that the new rules had several bad effects. Private investment and innovation were discouraged. They warned that it began a "costly and destructive era of government micromanagement." To them, the Open Internet Order and the Title II rules are a "giant step backwards for America's broadband networks and everyone who depends on them."

Current Challenges to Net Neutrality

The FCC's win in 2015 was not the end of the net neutrality debate in the United States. There have been many challenges to the new rules. Many Republican candidates running in the 2016 presidential election all promised to overturn the Open Internet Order. They call the change The Restoring Internet Freedom Act. This legislation would overturn the Open Internet Order. It would also keep similar rules from becoming law in the future.

The US Telecom Association filed a lawsuit on behalf of the telecommunications industry. It challenged the FCC's authority to regulate the internet. The association argues that the FCC overreached their power. They have power to regulate a "massive portion of the entire US economy." As of early 2016, the case was still open. The case could go on further with potential appeals in the Supreme Court.

Despite the neutrality rules in place, several companies have pursued zero-rating applications. Verizon introduced Go90. This is Verizon's own streaming video service that does not count against a user's data cap. Comcast has a similar service called Stream TV that zero-rates their content. AT&T began charging content providers fees so that their data did not count against a user's data plan. AT&T argued that the Open Internet Order does

The 2016 presidential candidates each have their own opinions on how the internet should be regulated in the United States.

not apply to mobile services. T-Mobile's Binge On product downgrades speeds for all video connections. They provide zero-ratings for specific companies, such as Netflix and Hulu. The FCC has not taken any action since there is no explicit ban on zero-rating in the Open Internet Order.

A Complicated Issue

The internet is everywhere and its uses expand every day. There is much at stake in the neutrality debate. It can decide how people communicate and interact online. The world's governments must balance regulation with economics. They must allow companies to pursue profits. At the same time, those companies must pursue profits without breaking the rules. ISPs and content providers cannot break their customers' trust.

In the future, consumers are likely to see increased monthly internet bills. Certain websites could suddenly become difficult to use. Or they might be even blocked entirely. One thing is certain. As time goes on, both supporters and opponents of net neutrality must stay vigilant in the ongoing battle for the Internet.

GLOSSARY

affiliation A close connection, often as a member, branch, or associate.

alienate To cause someone to feel isolated or estranged and become unsympathetic or hostile.

arbitrarily In a random manner.

bandwidth throttling The intentional slowing of internet service by an ISP to regulate network traffic and minimize bandwidth congestion.

concurrent Existing, happening, or done at the same time.

exempt Free from an obligation that applies to others.

Federal Communications Commission An independent US government agency that regulates radio, television, wire, satellite, and cable communications.

innovate To make changes in something established, especially by introducing new methods, ideas, or products.

internet service provider (ISP) A company that provides access to the internet, usually for a fee.

landline A cable laid across land that provides telecommunications.

network A number of interconnected computers, machines, or operations.

overblocking The practice of blocking legal websites in an effort to block illegal sites with similar addresses or hosted on related servers.

reclassify To assign to a different class or category.

safeguard To protect from harm or damage.

societal Relating to society or social relations.

stream A continuous flow of video and audio material transmitted or received over the internet.

telecommunications Communications or transmission of ideas by means of cable, telegraph, telephone, or broadcasting.

transparent Easily detected or understood.

FOR MORE INFORMATION

Berkman Center for Internet & Society
     23 Everett Street, 2nd Floor
     Cambridge, MA 02138
     (617) 495-754
     Website: https://cyber.law.harvard.edu
The Berkman Center for Internet & Society studies the dynamics and
     standards of cyberspace and possible laws to regulate it.

Center for Democracy & Technology
     1401 K Street NW, Floor 2
     Washington, DC 20005
     (202) 637-9800
     Website: https://cdt.org
The Center for Democracy & Technology (CDT) is a nonprofit organization
     that works to preserve the Internet and defend freedom of expression
     through the legal and political system.

Federal Communications Commission
     445 12th Street SW
     Washington, DC 20554
     (888) 225-5322
     Website: https://www.fcc.gov/
The Federal Communications Commission is an independent agency
     created by the US Congress to regulate radio, television, wire, satellite,
     and cable international communications.

IT World Canada, Inc.
    55 Town Centre Crt
    Toronto, ON M1P 4X4
    (416) 290-0240
    Website: http://www.itworldcanada.com/
IT World Canada provides multimedia information to Canadian
    technology professionals.

Pew Research Center, Internet & Tech
    1615 L Street, NW, Suite 800
    Washington, DC 20036
    (202) 419-4300
    Website: http://www.pewinternet.org
A nonpartisan resource, the Pew Research Center provides information to
    the public about current events, attitudes, and trends based on polling,
    demographic research, and media analysis.

Samuelson-Glushko Canadian Internet Policy & Public Interest Clinic
    (CIPPIC)
    University of Ottawa, Faculty of Law - Common Law Section
    57 Louis Pasteur St.
    Ottawa, Ontario, K1N 6N5
    (613) 562-5800 x2553
    E-mail: cippic@uottawa.ca
    Website: https://cippic.ca/en
The CIPPIC is a law and technology clinic that advocates in the public
    interest on technological issues and trains law students.

FOR FURTHER READING

Bily, Cynthia A. The Internet. Farmington Hills, MI: Greenhaven Press, 2012.

Bodden, Valerie. Using the Internet. Mankato, MN: Creative Education, 2013.

Brasch, Nicolas. The World Wide Web. South Melbourne, Australia: Nelson Cengage Learning, 2009.

Cosson, M. J., and Ronnie Rooney. The Smart Kid's Guide to Using the Internet. Mankato, MN: Child's World, 2015.

Döhmann, Indra Spiecker Genannt, and Jan Krämer. Network Neutrality and Open Access. Baden-Baden, Germany: Nomos, 2011.

Dougherty, Terri. Freedom of Expression and the Internet. Detroit, MI: Lucent Books, 2010.

Earl, C. F. Building a Business in the Virtual World. Broomall, PA: Mason Crest, 2014.

Fromm, Megan. How Policy and Profit Shape Content. New York, NY: Rosen, 2015.

Harvey, Damian, and Judy Brown. Tim Berners-Lee. London, England: Franklin Watts, 2014.

Macken, JoAnn Early, and William F. Pelgrin. Take a Closer Look at the Internet. South Egremont, MA: Red Chair Press, 2016.

McQuade, Samuel C., and Sarah Gentry. Living with the Internet. New York, NY: Chelsea House, 2012.

Porterfield, Jason. Tim Berners-Lee. New York, NY: Rosen, 2016.

Smibert, Angie. 12 Great Moments That Changed Internet History. St. Paul, MN: Black Rabbit Books, 2015.

Swanson, Jennifer, and Glen Mullaly. How the Internet Works. Mankato, MN: Child's World, 2012.

Wiener, Gary. The Internet. Farmington Hills, MI: Greenhaven Press, 2010.

BIBLIOGRAPHY

Bramoullé, Yann, Andrea Galeotti, and Brian W. Rogers. The Oxford Handbook of the Economics of Networks. New York, NY: Oxford University Press, 2016.

Chappell, Bill. "FCC Approves Net Neutrality Rules For 'Open Internet'" NPR. February 26, 2015 (http://www.npr.org/sections/thetwo-way/2015/02/26/389259382/net-neutrality-up-for-vote-today-by-fcc-board).

Deibert, Ronald, John Palfrey, Rafal Rohozinski, Jonathan Zittrain, and Janice Gross Stein. Access Denied: The Practice and Policy of Global Internet Filtering. Cambridge, MA: MIT Press, 2008.

Federal Communications Commission. "Internet Ecosystem Letter." TIA Online. December 10, 2014 (http://www.tiaonline.org/sites/default/files/pages/Internet_ecosystem_letter_FINAL_12.10.14.pdf).

McPherson, Stephanie Sammartino. Tim Berners-Lee: Inventor of the World Wide Web. Minneapolis, MN: Twenty-First Century Books, 2010.

Nowak, Peter. "Why 'Zero Rating' Is the New Battleground in Net Neutrality Debate." CBCnews. April 07, 2015 (http://www.cbc.ca/news/business/why-zero-rating-is-the-new-battleground-in-net-neutrality-debate-1.3015070).

Pogue, David. "The Net Neutrality Debate in 2 Minutes or Less." Scientific American. April 1, 2014 (http://www.scientificamerican.com/article/the-net-neutrality-debate-in-2-minutes-or-less).

Ruiz, Claudio. "Chile: First Country to Legislate Net Neutrality." Global Voices Overall RSS 20. Trans. Silvia Viñas. September 4, 2010 (https://globalvoices.org/2010/09/04/chile-first-country-to-legislate-net-neutrality).

VanHoose, David D. E-commerce Economics. New York, NY: Routledge, 2011.

Werbach, Kevin D. "Higher Standards: Regulation in the Network Age" Harvard Journal of Law and Technology. Vol. 23 (Fall 2009) (http://papers.ssrn.com/sol3/papers.cfm?abstract_id=1369962).

Zissis, Carin, and Rachel Glickhouse. "Net Neutrality Lessons from Latin America." US News. May 9, 2014 (http://www.usnews.com/opinion/blogs/world-report/2014/05/09/the-fcc-can-learn-some-net-neutrality-lessons-from-latin-america).

Websites

Because of the changing nature of internet links, Rosen Publishing has developed an online list of websites related to the subject of this book. This site is updated regularly. Please use this link to access this list:

http://www.rosenlinks.com/DIL/Net

INDEX

O

Obama, President Barack, 18, 33–34
Open Internet Order, 13–14, 33–38
opponents, of net neutrality, 18–22
O'Rielly, Michael, 36–37

P

Pai, Ajit, 36–37
Paul, Rand, 22

R

Reporters Without Borders, 3-–31
Republicans, 4, 32, 36
Restoring Freedom Act, The, 37
Roberts, Chief Justice John, 4

S

Sanders, Bernie, 18
Scalia, Justice Antonin, 4–5
Stream TV, 37
streaming media, 11, 17, 21, 36, 37
Sud, Veena, 36
Sununu, John, 37
supporters, of net neutrality, 15–18
Supreme Court, the, 4–5, 37

T

T-Mobile, 38
Telecom Regulatory Authority of India
    (TRAI), 28–29
Time Warner, 8
Title II, 34, 36, 37

U

US Congress, 22, 37
US Telecom Association, 37

V

Veach, Julie, 34
Verizon, 8, 22, 33–34, 37
viruses, 8

W

Warren, Elizabeth, 18
Weibo, 30–31
Wells, David, 17
Wheeler, Tom, 18, 22
Wireline Competition Bureau, 34
World Wide Web, 14, 25–26, 36

Y

YouTube, 18, 31

Z

zero-rating, 11, 25, 28, 37–38
Zuckerberg, Mark, 27–28

About the Author

Jeff Mapua is the author of several books on digital technology, including *Making the Most of Crowdfunding* and *A Career in Customer Service and Tech Support*. He has professional experience working in web-based technology and websites for national and global companies. Mapua lives in Dallas, Texas, with his wife, Ruby.

Photo Credits

Cover, p. 1 (left to right) Sommai/Shutterstock.com, Paul Matthew Photography/Shutterstock.com, ideyweb/Shutterstock.com, kittipong lukkhum/Shutterstock.com; p. 5 Brendan Smialowki/AFP/Getty Images; p. 7 leungchopan/Shutterstock.com; p. 9 goir/iStock/Thinkstock; p. 10 © iStockphoto.com/jetcityimage; p. 12 Alex Wong/Getty Images; p. 16 © iStockphoto.com/Hocus Focus Studio; p. 19 solopiero/iStock/Thinkstock; pp. 20, 38 Joseph Sohm/Shutterstock.com; p. 25 Catrina Genovese/ Hulton Archive/Getty Images; p. 27 © iStockphoto.com/EdStock; p. 28 Manjunath Kiran/AFP/Getty Images; p. 29 TonyV3112/Shutterstock.com; p. 33 Vacclav/Shutterstock.com; p. 35 © foto500/Shutterstock.com; cover and interior pages (pixels) © iStockphoto.com/suprun

Designer: Nicole Russo; Editor: Xina M. Uhl; Photo Researcher: Xina M. Uhl